Managing
Meltdowns

To understand is to empower!

Deborah

Managing Meltdowns

Using the S.C.A.R.E.D. Calming Technique
with Children and Adults with Autism

Deborah Lipsky and Will Richards

Jessica Kingsley Publishers
London and Philadelphia

First published in 2009
by Jessica Kingsley Publishers
116 Pentonville Road
London N1 9JB, UK
and
400 Market Street, Suite 400
Philadelphia, PA 19106, USA

www.jkp.com

Copyright © Deborah Lipsky and Will Richards 2009

Library of Congress Cataloging in Publication Data
Lipsky, Deborah.
    Managing meltdowns : using the S.C.A.R.E.D calming technique with children and adults with autism / Deborah Lipsky and Will Richards.
        p. ; cm.
    ISBN 978-1-84310-908-2 (pbk. : alk. paper) 1. Autism. 2. Crisis intervention (Mental health services) I. Richards, Will (William S.) II. Title.
    [DNLM: 1. Autistic Disorder--psychology. 2. Autistic Disorder--therapy. 3. Crisis Inter-vention--methods. WM 203.5 L767m 2009]
    RC553.A88L57 2009
    616.85'882--dc22

                                              2008025252

British Library Cataloguing in Publication Data
A CIP catalogue record for this book is available from the British Library

ISBN 978 1 84310 908 2

Printed and bound in the United States by
Thomson-Shore, 7300 Joy Road, Dexter, MI 48130

Contents

Foreword

The orange design on the cover of this book is significant in that orange is recognized as the universal color of distress. Meltdowns are extremely distressing to the person experiencing them as well as those witnessing the event. This book, with its orange design, is readily identified as an emergency resource and easily accessed when needed. That is also why the acronym, S.C.A.R.E.D., is apt. Fear is the primary affect experienced by all involved when meltdowns occur.

Because meltdowns are distressing to all involved, there is often a sense of urgency to develop an intervention plan. The prioritized sequence for intervention is encoded in the acronym. The first priority is to provide safety (SAFE), followed by a sense of calm (CALM), and so forth. Only after assessment of SCARE are we ready to focus on D (DEVELOP A PLAN). We caution against the temptation to develop a plan before thoroughly addressing the other elements encapsulated in the S.C.A.R.E.D. acronym.

Most written material regarding autism is composed by neurotypical (non-autistic) individuals with a somewhat limited perspective. This has resulted in portraying autistic learning styles as dysfunctional. A new and more fruitful approach is currently gaining acceptance in the

United Kingdom. This conceptualization accepts an autistic cognitive style as different, with different gifts and different limitations.

A focus on different interest systems and different allocation of attention has provided a fresh approach to understanding autism. Central to this approach are the concepts of *monotropism* and *polytropism*, terms coined by Lesser and Murray (Lesser, M.J. and Murray, D.K.C. (1998) "Mind as a dynamical system." Durham International Conference on Psychobiology of Autism: Current Research and Practice). "-tropism" is derived from the Greek "*trepo*" meaning turn. *Monotropism* is the turning toward one interest to the exclusion of others. *Polytropism* is maintaining of several interests simultaneously.

Each person's perception of the world is the result of a combination of biologically determined ways of understanding the world, and personal history or experience. Several writers, such as Attwood, Grinker, Grandin and Johnson, and Greenspan and Wieder, have expounded on the different learning styles that are based on individual differences in perception.

The commoner of these two cognitive styles, polytropism, is sometimes called "neurotypical" (NT) and involves the ability to integrate various perceptual modalities at one time, to multitask, to modulate emotional reactions, and to keep in mind the perspectives of others in a group without losing one's own perspective. This cognitive style is *polytropic.*

Conformity is a value in the society at large and measures are taken to ensure that individuals are socialized in a way that forms commonality of thought, perceptions, emotional expression, and behavior in general. Sharing that commonality, it is relatively easy for likeminded individuals to predict the thoughts and actions of others. Projecting one's own thoughts and feelings onto others is the basis for NT notions of empathy and theory of mind. Neurotypical individuals gain a sense of safety and control from their common social networks.

The autistic cognitive style is *monotropic.* Monotropic interests are narrow, deep, nonsocial, and unconnected to each other. They are generally individually aroused and involve unitasking. Autistic individuals gain a sense of safety and control from mastery and gathering of information in their areas of interest.

Because of the differing cognitive style autistics present, some commonly used interventions during times of distress, crisis, trauma, or chaos can be inappropriate and can lead to worsening of difficulties rather than providing relief. Some techniques commonly recommended, like maintaining eye contact and using light touch, can be counterproductive when used with autistic individuals.

The purpose of this manual is to help explain the autistic experience and mindset and to guide the interventions of first responders. There are several models for crisis intervention including the MANDT (designed by David H. Mandt, Sr.) and NAPPI (Non Abusive Psychological and Physical Intervention) systems. This manual is not meant to supplant those, but rather to supplement existing training.

THE DEVELOPMENT OF THE S.C.A.R.E.D. MODEL

Deb Lipsky and Will Richards met in the spring of 2005. Deb had recently been diagnosed as autistic after living in semi-seclusion for the previous eighteen years on a farm in rural Aroostook County, Maine, near the Canadian border. After being diagnosed she decided to return to the work force. She asked herself what sort of job would be suitable for an autistic woman in her forties. The only autistic person she was familiar with was Temple Grandin, so she decided that she would become a national speaker. Although she had a Masters degree in counseling and education, she lacked the social skills required to interact with an audience. She took Bard training to learn the art of verbal communication. Based on that, she offered her services to a nation-wide seminar company and was given a try. She was an instant success, but difficulties with transitions and changes led to an increase in meltdowns which jeopardized her career plans. She also was involved as a board member and educator for the Autism Society of Maine.

Will Richards had his first clinical experience working with autistic individuals in the 1960s as a graduate student at Arizona State University. After teaching at Western Illinois University and having various clinical/administrative positions at institutional and community-based programs he went into private practice. For the past eight years he has worked exclusively with individuals on the autism spectrum. While working with adults who ranged from needing 24-hour supervision to well-established professionals, he encountered the usual communication and socialization challenges, but commonly found the most pressing issue was unwanted meltdowns. The Autism Society of Maine frequently called on him to provide diagnostic clarification, therapy, and consultation.

It was through the Autism Society of Maine that Deb and Will met. They initially met to discuss current research and practice in social skills training, but quickly focused on communication differences. Miscommunication between the two was an initial obstacle. Will had a terrible propensity to talk in metaphor while Deb used literal language. As long as language was literal there was no miscommunication. They worked out a routine for clarification that became the basis for their workshops on communication.

Less than six months after meeting, but before Deb was to go on the road as a national speaker, they were scheduled to do their first full-day workshop. The workshop was to be held in Brewer, ME, across the Penobscot River from Bangor. Deb had a motel room in Brewer but the night before went to Bangor to pick up a few things. She was not accustomed to the lights and sounds of the night so parked her car and began to walk. Deb finds walking and being near water calming which works well in Linneus, ME, but not so well on a cold November night in Bangor. She was not dressed for the cold and after walking many miles up and down the river she found herself at the river's edge in the dark. At about 9pm Will called to check on her to find that she had no idea of how to get back to her car. Stressed from the cold she became more worried about getting back to Brewer when she came to a chain link fence with the sign, NO TRESPASSING, VIOLATORS WILL BE PROSECUTED. Her phone was going dead, nobody knew where exactly she was, she was shivering, and her thinking was cloudy. She was beginning to meltdown and decided that the way to get back was to swim across the river. The river is a tidal river, wide and fast and Deb was not a swimmer. After another two harrowing hours and with the help of the Bangor police she was found and disaster was averted. Deb was remorseful and was convinced she had ruined a collegial relationship. This turned out not to be the case.

Instead it was the beginning of a mutually beneficial exploration into the nature of meltdowns. Will was very aware of some of the misconceptions regarding meltdowns and the resulting conflicts between those intervening. Deb was able to describe in detail what her experience was like as an autistic person with frequent meltdowns. Working together on this project was mutually affirming.

Deb and Will enthusiastically embarked on challenging existing stereotypes on meltdowns. Meltdowns have been commonly referred to as temper tantrums with resultant inappropriate interventions. It became apparent that what was needed was a clear understanding of meltdowns and guidelines for intervening. They created intervention strategies and began to do seminars and workshops. Meltdowns are scary for those experiencing them and those witnessing them. When one is scared the best choices are not made. The acronym S.C.A.R.E.D. allowed for an easy to remember guide for implementation of intervention strategies.

You are invited to visit Deb and Will's website at:
www.lipskyrichardsautism.com

Introduction

What do you think of when you hear "autism"? Do you picture a young child sitting and rocking in a corner of the room, oblivious to the world around him or her? Perhaps you think of Dustin Hoffman in his portrayal of "Rainman" in the movie of that name. While both images are correct, they are only two faces of autism: autism presents differently in each individual. Society depicts autism as a disorder, but at its core, it is a neurological difference in how we perceive the world around us. Autistic individuals have many unique gifts and talents. Albert Einstein, Thomas Edison, and Mozart are just a few individuals who would probably be classified as high-functioning autistic individuals today.

With these gifts come some limitations. One of these limitations is termed a catastrophic reaction or "meltdown". It is not a temper tantrum. To the outside world, catastrophic reactions look appalling and much more frightening than they actually are. The key is to understand how an autistic individual perceives danger and to react in such a way as to de-escalate the situation. We are not crazy, nor do we have control, when an overload occurs in our brain. We need your intervention and help to stay safe when such a crisis happens.

I have created an ER (emergency room) training program to teach hospital staff how to intervene when autistic individuals are in crisis. As a former reserve police officer, emergency medical technician, and firefighter, I have an understanding of that perspective. I also have high-functioning autism and have a deep understanding of the autistic perspective. The anecdotes that I give relate to the concepts presented. Another autistic individual would give very different examples, but the same principles apply.

My colleague, Will Richards, Ph.D., a psychologist who has worked extensively with autistic individuals, created an acronym, S.C.A.R.E.D., that has general application for intervening with autistic individuals in crisis. We have collaborated on this manual to bring our combined knowledge together in such as way as to bring greater awareness for first responders in understanding autism and in employing appropriate interventions.

Autistic individuals are members of every community and have more frequent contact with first responders than the general population. The typical contact is when the individual is experiencing a catastrophic reaction. Unfortunately one does not get a second chance to make a first impression. The current mindset of first responders is on targeted populations such as terrorists, drug users and traffickers, and sex offenders (especially pedophiles). Autistic individuals may be mis-identified as any of the above. As a first responder it is critical to make an accurate assessment of each situation.

We hope that you will use this manual as a reference guide, keeping a copy on hand to refer to whenever you come in contact with autistic individuals.

Note: This manual is intended solely as a guide. Information in this manual is general in nature. The autistic community is diverse and there is no substitute for accurate information about each individual. The most pertinent information comes from the individual himself/herself and from those with the closest relationship to him/her.

CATASTROPHIC REACTIONS

Autistic individuals tend to use one sensory channel at a time. We do not readily integrate information from other senses. Autistic individuals view the world as chaotic and unpredictable. Many of us have heightened sense capabilities, such as being able to see the 60 pulses per second that a fluorescent light emits, or hear things almost undetectable to others around. There are those who have heightened smell or touch sensitivities too. These types of hypersensitivities create hypervigilance and startle responses.

Imagine if you had to see fluorescent lighting in this way or not be able to shut out noises all around you every minute of your life. Wouldn't there come a breaking point for you? For people with autism it is called "sensory overload" where the brain needs a little "down time" to regroup. It is essentially a catastrophic reaction to overstimulation. Sensory overload will present itself differently for each individual but the commonality here is the sense of panic it creates within the autistic person's mind. It is a completely terrifying experience for me and for other autistic individuals. Progressive shutting down of sensory systems, the narrowing of perception, and the loss of the ability to communicate at the most basic level, is what we experience, and it can be terrifying.

Catastrophic reactions present very differently for different individuals. Remember that fear is a primary emotional response of autistic individuals. Often the initial physical response is to freeze. Sometimes a stressor elicits a freeze response where we can't respond to the stressor in any adaptive way at all. We are just "frozen in our tracks" and cannot respond to verbal orders. Sometimes this freezing is cognitive and we are unable to gain a different perspective. Oftentimes the freeze response is physical and we are unable to respond to verbal commands. At other times the freeze response is followed by a flight response.

The flight response may occur even if a verbal warning is given. This can lead to a disaster if the warning is "Stop or I will shoot!" If a flight response is not available, an individual may become combative if approached or forcibly restrained. This is an even less safe situation for all concerned.

Commonly misperceived autistic coping strategies

Since autistic individuals perceive the world as chaotic, one method to keep things predictable and to hold this fear of losing control at bay is to create routines and rituals which provide a sense of security. During times of stress these rituals and routines will increase in an attempt to control the chaos around them. It is a common coping strategy for autistic individuals to return them to their normalcy. This may be misperceived as being willful, noncompliant, and uncooperative. Sometimes autistic individuals script responses to perceived threats. This can be a huge problem when the script does not match the situation, e.g. attempting to disarm an individual coming at you with a drawn gun.

Another way in which individuals with autism try to feel safe is by self-stimulation, also known as "self-stimming". Behaviors such as hand-flapping, rocking, leg-shaking, clutching or handling an object, and talking out loud to one's self are just a few ways to self-stim.

Anxious states/catastrophic reactions occur primarily due to:

1. sudden change, being taken by surprise, being caught off guard

2. not understanding the reason for sudden change

3. people in authority failing to explain, carefully, sequentially, and descriptively what will be happening in any situation

4. someone failing to respond to an autistic individual's questions in conrete, literal fashion

5. sensory overload

6. being asked to multitask or to integrate multiple sensory inputs.

Keep in mind that during periods of extreme stress or catastrophic reactions:

1. Individuals might have a limited awareness of aspects of their surroundings.

2. Individuals might have an increased focus on seemingly trivial aspects of their surroundings.

3. Very little that is said will be processed.

4. Attempts to communicate nonverbally will not be received or will be misperceived.

5. Individuals are at an increased risk of harming themselves due to impaired reasoning abilities.

6. Individuals are at an increased risk of being harmed by others due to misunderstanding of their behavior.

7. Individuals may exhibit an instinctual fear, flight, or freeze response of self-preservation by becoming combative if forcibly restrained or approached.

When intervening with an individual who is experiencing a catastrophic reaction, the first concern should be the safety of the individual and those around him/her. It is important for first responders and others to be able to differentiate a catastrophic response from a temper tantrum and to respond to it appropriately. The major precipitating affect is terror and the behavior is not manipulative. We used the acronym S.C.A.R.E.D. to focus on the affective state and the appropriate responses to it.

S.C.A.R.E.D.

S Safe: The initial focus should be to provide an environment that is safe and secure.

Don't try to restrain the individual.

Don't leave him/her alone.

Do remove unwanted stimulation or guide the individual to a less stimulating environment.

Do remove social pressure from the situation.

C Calm: Remain calm; there is no need for you to be out of control. Use concrete or literal language that is descriptive and not evaluative.

Don't try to "process" what has happened or is happening.

Do talk in a strong, calm and reassuring voice.

A Affirmation: Provide validation of affect and acknowledge that the individual is doing the best he/she can to resolve the situation.

Don't ask unnecessary questions or challenge responses.

Do refer to the individual by name and acknowledge his/her fear.

R Routine: The individual's comfort zone is far more likely to be in his/her repetition of routines.

Don't attempt to interfere with harmless routines like repetitive statements or walking in figure eights.

Do

- reflect his/her behavior and perception
- encourage his/her routine
- provide environmental supports for his/her routines
- offer reassurance.

Only after the catastrophic reaction is over, help the individual repair the situation.

E Empathy: Understand from the autistic individual's perspective.

Don't lecture about the effect his/her behavior is having on others.

Don't humiliate or shame.

Do acknowledge his/her fear and show that you are there to support him/her and not to make him/her do something he/she does not understand.

D Develop an intervention strategy: An intervention plan reduces the frequency, duration, intensity, and negative outcomes of meltdowns

Don't rely on a generic strategy.

Don't develop a strategy without thorough consultation with the individual and his/her family.

Do work with the individual to develop concrete behavioral strategies for assisting during a meltdown.

Frequently Asked Questions

In addition to traveling the United States and Canada doing different seminars on autism from an insider's perspective, Deb frequently teams up with Will to run a six-hour training workshop in implementing the S.C.A.R.E.D. model for understanding and managing meltdowns. During these sessions, they have received countless questions concerning meltdowns. Here are some of the more frequently asked questions.

WHAT IS A MELTDOWN?

It is an extreme emotional/behavioral response to stress or overstimulation. It is triggered by a "fight or flight" response, which releases adrenaline into the body, creating heightened anxiety and causing the individual to switch to an instinctual survival mode. This is a common human reaction to stress. In autistic individuals, this fight or flight response is commonly seen as either bolting away from a situation or striking out. While it has a protective function in reaction to internal or external overstimulation, it can have unfortunate consequences. It can be accompanied by cognitive impairment, perceptual distortion, and narrowing of sensory experience.

DO ALL AUTISTIC PEOPLE EXPERIENCE MELTDOWNS IN THE SAME WAY?

No, every individual is different. How people react to overwhelming stress is influenced by factors such as living environment, upbringing and cultural differences. This is true of autistic individuals as well. The observed behavior of an autistic individual may vary from situation to situation.

WHAT ARE COMMON FEATURES OF MELTDOWNS?

1. They are due to overwhelming stimulation.

2. They are caused by sensory or cognitive overload, sometimes in conjunction with each other.

3. Novel situations or sudden change can elicit a meltdown.

4. Transitions (i.e. going from class to class, change in topic, change in supervisor, etc.) frequently set the stage for meltdowns.

5. All meltdowns are a reaction to severe stress, although the stress may not be readily apparent to an observer.

6. There will be cognitive dysfunction.

7. Individuals will likely become hyposensitive or hypersensitive to pain.

8. After the meltdown phase there are frequently intense feelings of shame, remorse, and humiliation. There is a frequent fear that relationships have been harmed beyond repair.

9. Meltdowns are time limited.

WHAT CAUSES A MELTDOWN OR CATASTROPHIC REACTION?

There are many factors that could cause a meltdown or catastrophic reaction, but primarily they occur because the autistic person:

1. does not understand the reason for sudden change

2. does not receive understandable answers to questions

3. is taken by surprise

4. has a sensory overload

5. is given too many choices

6. is given open-ended or vaguely defined tasks.

WHAT ARE SOME OF THE WARNING SIGNS OF A POTENTIAL MELTDOWN?

Remember that during the meltdown phases the fight or flight response is accompanied by a release of adrenaline, which heightens fear or anxiety. Keep in mind that many autistic individuals get frustrated and angry but are unable to communicate the reasons for their emotions. These feelings are frequently expressed nonverbally. You will see many of these reactions:

1. pacing back and forth or in circles

2. increasing self-stimulatory behaviors (for example, flapping hands)

3. perseverating on one topic

4. repeating words or phrases over and over (echolalia)

5. experiencing difficulty answering questions (cognitive breakdown)

6. stuttering or showing pressured speech

7. extreme resistance to disengaging from a ritual or routine

8. becoming mute.

YOU INTERCHANGE "MELTDOWN" AND "CATASTROPHIC REACTION". ARE THEY THE SAME?

Temple Grandin uses the term "catastrophic reaction" to refer to meltdowns. Many people use the terms interchangeably. Deb makes a distinction between stressful events and overwhelming sensory situations that gradually build up to the point that they can no longer be tolerated and those events marked by a sudden change resulting in a sudden reaction. For her the reaction to prolonged stress is a meltdown. For example, Deb finds busy airports with noisy people, long waits, unfamiliar sounds, bright lights etc. extremely stressful. She is aware of the stress but has coping strategies. If the stress is prolonged she may spiral into a meltdown. It involves the gradual build-up of stress without adequate pressure release, much like a nuclear power plant meltdown! For Deb, a sudden change when things are going according to script – for example the unexpected cancellation of a connecting flight – triggers an immediate and extreme reaction she terms a "catastrophic reaction".

ARE MELTDOWNS AND TEMPER TANTRUMS THE SAME THING?

Absolutely not. Tantrums are goal-directed behavior. They are intended to manipulate another individual into doing something. They involve premeditation and planning to achieve an outcome. Meltdowns are uncontrolled reactions to overwhelming stress.

WHY IS THERE A HIGH RISK OF INJURY DURING A MELTDOWN?

When autistic individuals are experiencing a meltdown they are functioning in a primitive self-preservation mode. Cognitive functioning is greatly impaired. The risk of self-injury increases due to a lack of awareness of surroundings, a high pain threshold and physical fatigue. Attempts to escape may lead to exposure to other dangers. Running water attracts many autistic individuals and accidental injury and drowning are major causes of death. Self-injurious behavior such as head banging is very common during meltdowns.

Physical restraint used during meltdowns is another cause of injury. Many autistic individuals have died while being restrained.

CAN CAREFUL PLANNING AND SCRIPTING PREVENT ALL MELTDOWNS?

Unfortunately the answer is "no". There are events and circumstances beyond our control. We can never be totally prepared despite the best-laid plans. However, careful planning and scripting is extremely beneficial in decreasing the probability of meltdowns in many situations. It is helpful to have a back-up plan (a "Plan B") should the primary plan go off script. Scripts are very important for autistic individuals. Advance notice of novel situations helps the autistic individual prepare for that event.

ARE THERE DIFFERENT TYPES OF MELTDOWNS?

Most certainly. The most familiar are the outward explosive behaviors that draw a lot of attention. Some autistic individuals disengage or "shut down" and withdraw from the world around them. Sometimes this involves physical withdrawal to another place. Sometimes it involves limiting communication or becoming mute. While a shutdown presents very differently from the more attention-drawing meltdown, it is important to remember that the same factors that contribute to meltdowns also contribute to shutdowns.

DEB, WHAT DO YOU EXPERIENCE WHEN YOU HAVE A MELTDOWN?

I experience different things depending on whether it is a sensory-based or a cognitive-based meltdown. During a sensory meltdown I feel like I am crawling out of my skin. All I feel is intense pressure like I'm about to explode. I feel a need to escape. If I cannot escape, I eventually go into a blackout phase. Subsequently I have no memory of this phase. Recovery is gradual. For a cognitive meltdown, my brain is trying out possible explanations to situations and communication attempts I cannot understand. I try to script out responses to each and every alternative I can imagine. Failure to get clarification leads to erroneous assumptions which overload my thought processes. I sense the brain shutting down but my body is winding up. When I try to compensate for that my speech becomes pressured or I stutter, increasing my frustration. I eventually am not able to communicate at all. I become terrified and desperate which leads to further spiraling. At that point I am in full meltdown with no control.

DEB, WHAT WOULD YOU SAY IS THE MOST DIFFICULT PART FOR YOU DURING THIS TIME?

The entire meltdown phase for me is difficult and each aspect brings its own unique challenges. I think the most difficult thing I experience is the reaction or disbelief of others around me. Because I am successful, social, and an adult, people can quickly forget that I am still autistic. Because I look "normal" (no visible handicap) it is common for me not to be believed when I explain that I am autistic and having difficulty with a situation. Many times in high-stress situations where I can't exit or relieve the stressors I am told to "hold it together", or "grow up" or rely on my personal strategies to deal with the anxiety. It is extremely frustrating because I have done that already but the situation is too difficult for me to handle. I can only bear sensory overloads for a certain period of time before my body will instinctively react adversely to them. I am told to "learn to control it" at times when it is impossible to do so, but it is expected of me because I am an adult. There is this unrealistic expectation that we need to eradicate our autistic nature as we become adults. I have had many "friends" who, after witnessing a meltdown or two, decided to end the friendship because they can't "deal" with it. It is expected that autistic children learn to adapt to a non-autistic society's way of life. As children grow into adulthood they develop positive coping strategies to deal with everyday struggles but they are still autistic and things will go off script at one time or another, catching them by surprise. As adults it is unacceptable to others for them to exhibit the extreme emotional and behavioral response of a meltdown.

IS THERE ANYTHING ELSE I CAN DO WHEN I AM WITH AN AUTISTIC INDIVIDUAL TO HELP REDUCE THE LIKELIHOOD OF A MELTDOWN IN PUBLIC?

One of the most helpful things you can do is to anticipate some of the difficulties that individual may encounter. For instance, Deb has sensory issues regarding large crowds. If a friend is visiting for the holiday weekend, Deb may suggest that they go Christmas shopping the day after Thanksgiving which, in the United States, marks the Christmas shopping season and is the busiest shopping day of the year. Deb may not have thought of the pushy crowds, noises, and smells, as well as parking constraints, long queue lines, etc. It would be helpful for Deb's friend to point out the difficulties they may encounter before going and suggest something different.

CAN A TEMPER TANTRUM DEVELOP INTO A MELTDOWN?

Autistic individuals as well as anyone else can display both temper tantrums and meltdowns. Temper tantrums, depending on how they are handled, can lead to meltdowns.

ARE THERE ANY PHRASES I SHOULD AVOID THAT MAY TRIGGER A MELTDOWN RESPONSE?

Yes. Autistic people need concrete timeframes and are very literal. Phrases such as "we'll see", "maybe", "if you are good", "later", "what do you want to do?", "I'll be back shortly", "I'll only be a minute", "wait a second", and so on, offer no concrete set timescales and make it impossible for an autistic individual to plan a scenario. These comments can be a source of great anxiety and may precipitate a meltdown.

Also, autistic individuals may place distinct meanings on particular words or have a history where a word or phrase has signaled negative consequences. In some instances, referring to an individual by his proper name, for example "William" instead of "Will", may be enough to trigger a response.

When an individual is asked to modify a routine or do something out of the ordinary, the request is frequently followed by a barrage of questions. Seemingly endless "What if… ?" questions are asked. This is an attempt to get clarification so that a new scenario can be scripted. The greater the anxiety, the more detail is needed to provide manageable timeframes and back-up plans.

YOU MENTIONED A FREEZE RESPONSE. WHAT IS THAT AND WHY IS IT IMPORTANT?

A freeze response occurs when an individual is startled and unable to assess the situation. It is much like a deer caught in the headlights. Many times the freeze response occurs when an individual does not understand the intent of a question. If a question is vague, uses metaphors, or is modified by voice inflection or gestures, it commonly leads to a freeze. Sometimes a freeze looks like a blank stare and sometimes it is even misdiagnosed as a partial complex seizure. It is a critical time for preventing a meltdown. Sometimes the individual is badgered by additional similar questions further complicating the miscommunication. What is needed is clarification, asking what was heard and how it was perceived. A freeze response, if not clarified, can frequently lead to a shutdown or meltdown.

Safe

For people with autism safety is an omnipresent concern. Finding a safe place, physically and psychologically, is, for many autistic individuals, a constant struggle. Fear is the predominant emotional state experienced. Auditory processing problems lead to incompletely understood instructions and missed warnings. A narrow focus leads to missing the larger picture and this frequently leads to unsafe situations. Breaking unwritten social rules and experiencing unwritten negative consequences are especially frustrating and can lead to being unsafe from bullying and worse. Miscommunication can lead to exploitation. Novel situations frequently become unsafe situations. Unsafe situations can lead to catastrophic reactions. Catastrophic reactions are sometimes preventable and reversible. They are always self-limiting.

Transitions frequently are the most unsafe situations. These include forced transitions in thought as well as in physical location. Shifting of focus does not come quickly and, when forced, causes a diminished sense of safety and security.

Many times a safe place is sought out if a situation is perceived as threatening. What appears to be running away is often running for security. When overwhelmed, an autistic individual may be focused only on returning home. Home may be hundreds of miles away. Sometimes safety is experienced by curling up in a bedroom closet. At times this is not a good choice, but because of a narrowing perception and lessening cognitive abilities this is the only option considered. Safety is not found in numbers. Safety is found in order, predictability, and routine.

Neurotypicals find safety in a mindset of general preparedness. Autistics often are the safest individuals in potentially risky situations that require a strict adherence to protocol. They are frequently good at detail but sometimes miss the big picture. They do not develop a general concept of safety, but rather develop specific safe procedures for specific situations. They may be very exacting with regard to taking medication, but fail to recognize that they are becoming exhausted or on the verge of hypothermia.

To ask autistic individuals if they are safe or if they feel safe is much too vague, especially if they are experiencing or have just experienced a meltdown. Individuals may feel safe holding on to a favorite possession but may be totally unaware of current dangerous situations. They also may believe they are safe because they have decided on a course of action, being unaware of unintended results. Reliance on others is necessary for safety when experiencing catastrophic reactions. This means that individuals should not be left alone until it is certain that they have a workable plan.

Safety begins with ensuring the safety of all during the meltdown, but it does not end there. The post-meltdown phase presents its own risks. Often the individual is feeling ashamed and confused. Post meltdown, support and affirmation are critical. For autistic individuals, safety is not a unitary concept. Dozens or even hundreds of safety plans are needed. A safety plan for dealing with an online scam will be very different from a safety plan for medication compliance, and so on and on.

The following section describes only a plan for what *I* need in a situation that others can navigate with ease. It is not meant to be an appropriate plan for anyone but me. Some autistic individuals could safely handle this task—but not other tasks that I can handle easily. It does provide an example of the need to give guidelines for situations where we might become overwhelmed. It may also give you the appreciation of how difficult it is to develop strategies for preparing for novel situations.

JOB DESCRIPTION FOR TRAVEL COMPANION

For the past year I have achieved considerable success as a national speaker. From my presence during workshops nobody could imagine the difficulties I can encounter with transitions. The easy part is my presentation, although I am exhausted after it is over.

The challenge is getting from my home in Linneus, Maine, to the site of the presentation and back again safely. Other more manageable challenges involve unstructured break and lunch activities, as well as novel situations which catch me off guard.

I have come to realize that I cannot anticipate and script all possible transitional difficulties. For that reason I need a travel companion. In the course of the past year I have learned which travel companions work well.

The companions that I have had the most success with are those who do not need to be the center of attraction. They act more like a personal secretary or personal assistant. They do not seek the limelight. Their only role is to see that I get to and return from my destination safely. With the right companion, travel can be easy and thoroughly enjoyable. Difficult situations can be anticipated and managed before meltdowns occur. Even in those situations where unrelenting sensory stimulation leads to a meltdown, companions familiar with strategies for dealing with meltdowns know that they are time-limited and relatively easy to manage.

I need to feel free to express my thoughts and feelings. My companion needs to be honest with me as well. Nothing destroys trust as much as duplicity, hidden agendas, or dishonesty. It is important that the assistant adapts to my schedules and does not try to fit me into his or hers.

Remaining calm in challenging situations is another important characteristic for a traveling companion. As a registered guide I know that my clients do not need to worry unless I lose control. Some individuals are just not suited to be a traveling assistant because of their tendency to panic or become hysterical.

Critical companions do not make good travel companions. During transitions I have trouble processing new information. Positive affirmation is especially important at these times and this seems to come more naturally for some people than others. It is a bad time to correct a minor social *faux pas*. The time to process what I could have done differently is often days later. It is also a bad time to make commitments. Often I am deluged after a workshop by people wanting to talk with me. It is important that my assistant help at these times with packing up, making copies of the evaluations, and monitoring that people do not all swamp me and cause sensory overload.

Like most autistic individuals I have a few routines that are important to me in maintaining a sense of safety. My routines are pretty innocuous but if they are challenged or interrupted, it can be quite distressing. Accommodation to my routines is easy.

It is important for my traveling companion to have empathy and understand my perspective. I need to know his/her perspective or mindset as well. For this reason I cannot employ someone at the last minute who does not know autism or me.

If I feel beleaguered or badgered my first tendency is to escape, but being alone is not a good alternative. I tend to endure discomfort rather than inconvenience anyone. It took quite a while before I was able to request a bathroom stop, but being able to do that has made life a lot easier. I need to teach my traveling companion the signs that I am becoming distressed so that I can easily calm myself and/or he/she can help me calm down. I need to review and practice my intervention plan for meltdowns with my traveling companion so he/she will intervene appropriately and with confidence.

SAFE

What first responders should *not* do

✗ Do not attempt to restrain a highly agitated individual. Many have a hyposensitive pain response. They do not initially feel physical pain because their sensory systems have begun to shut down. There have been reports of autistic individuals being killed as a result of asphyxiation while being restrained. Use restraint as a last resort.

✗ Do not ask open-ended questions. "Are you OK? Do you need help? What do you want me to do? Are you sure you are safe now?"

✗ Do not present with a show of force.

What first responders *should* do

✔ Initial attempts should be made to defuse the situation. Reduce the level of sensory stimulation. Remain calm. You are intervening on behalf of a terrified person who needs your help and understanding, not an aggressive, violent person.

✔ Try to determine if the individual is injured. Many autistic individuals have a high threshold for pain and during a meltdown may be unaware that they have a serious injury.

✔ Maintain a calm social presence. Never leave an individual experiencing a catastrophic reaction unattended.

✔ Talk directly to the individual experiencing a catastrophic reaction. Provide consistent, reassuring, declarative statements. Use the person's name when addressing him/her. Let the person know that your role is to provide a safe environment until he/she has recovered.

✔ Determine if the individual has identification and an intervention plan.

✔ Take a submissive stance. Approach in a non-threatening manner, avoiding quick movements and unwanted touch.

✔ If the situation is chaotic with several interveners, announce that you have an understanding of autism and ask others to step back and remain quiet.

✔ Before leaving an individual, ask him/her to describe in detail what he/she is going to do and within what timeframe.

✔ Refer to the individual's plan and do not leave him/her alone until the plan has been followed.

Strategies autistic individuals can employ to be safe

1. Get to know first responders in your community and make them aware of your plan.

2. Carry identification, which also includes a contact list.

3. Develop a personalized intervention plan and carry it with you.

4. Wear a med alert or a personal location device.

Calm

For most autistic individuals, fear is their primary emotion. They experience frequent negative consequences in social situations. Their behavior is misinterpreted and punished. Their social world is chaotic, with unpredictable pain. Autistic individuals frequently worry, especially about social situations, because they have so little control over outcomes. They have a history of being told they do things wrong more often than they are told they do things right. They are told that they are selfish and self-centered.

When neurotypicals (NTs) worry, they usually seek out the counsel of other NTs. When autistics worry, they have limited means of cognitively relieving their worries. They often do not have a close friend to ask personal questions. They often worry about the unwritten rules of social conduct but have trouble determining what those rules are, although neurotypicals seem to just know. There are also unwritten consequences for not following unwritten rules. Sometimes reading books or watching movies is recommended as a way to learn social appropriateness. Often this is unhelpful or even counterproductive.

Social gatherings can be extremely difficult and remaining calm is a huge challenge. Talking to NTs can be stressful because of the difficulty understanding nuances, sarcasm, hidden meanings, and hidden agendas.

Even special interests, which may be experienced as exhilarating, often are rudely interrupted. This can be extremely disorienting and aversive. Those activities that autistic individuals find pleasurable are often the ones that the NT world considers dysfunctional. Interruption of passionate interests can lead to a feeling of extreme distress, helplessness and hopelessness. In extreme cases this leads to a kind of fatalism or "What's the use?"

Calmness, not to be confused with the ecstasy or exhilaration experienced when engaging in special interests, is a prized but rare commodity. Calmness is required to process events more effectively. NTs often process information from multiple sources rapidly. For autistics information is often restricted to one channel at a time and can only be processed after the event. Too often, autistic individuals are overwhelmed with information when they are least able to process it, as when in crisis. During a meltdown, or shortly after, information cannot be processed. Often memory of the event is poor. Following a catastrophic reaction, the emotional experience is often an intense sense of shame or humiliation. This is also not to be confused with calmness.

Sometimes, the only option is to resort to alcohol or other drugs in an attempt to relieve stress. This only leads to other sources of stress, but the need to relieve stress is so great that the long-term effects are not considered. Dependence on legal and sometimes illegal substances is common in the autistic community.

Sometimes during periods of unremitting over-stimulation or stress, the only calm considered is death.

Some autistic individuals think about death a lot and many commit suicide. The suicide rate for autistic individuals is not known for sure, but many epidemiologists suggest that it is high.

We do find calmness in different ways. For each autistic individual, calmness is achieved somewhat differently. We sometimes find sensory stimulation calming. For some of us the touch of fur or watching running water is calming. Sometimes we are most calm when we are alone. Many of us prefer the dark, or at least avoid bright light. Deep pressure is often calming. Temple Grandin, a well-known autistic woman, developed a squeeze machine which exerted a deep pressure on her body (see Grandin, T. (1995) *Thinking in Pictures*. New York: Doubleday). Many other autistic individuals have developed their unique means of attaining deep pressure. Some wear very tight clothing, some carry heavy backpacks, some wear flak jackets or other weighted apparel. Some people seek strong hugs, although this can be dangerous. We need to be careful when we ask for a firm hug, because we may be sending the wrong message.

The restoration of a sense of inner calm appears to me to be a universal desire. As individuals, we each find our own way that works to quell the anxiety that at times overpowers us. What works for one individual does not necessarily work for someone else. It is important to tailor calming methods to the person's needs and desires. I have been told that yoga is a great way to calm the restlessness inside of us, yet I have tried yoga and all it did was increase anxiety, because I am not well coordinated and struggled just to keep my balance. For others it may be just the answer.

For me the old saying that "Necessity is the mother of invention" really was illustrated when I came across a calming technique totally by accident.

I suffer from asthma, and one day the respiratory therapist was trying to illustrate what an asthma attack was like by having me breathe through a straw. This demontration did not mimic my asthma attacks. I needed to come up with another technique that better mimicked the constriction I feel when I try to inhale during an asthma attack. I could then come up with compensating strategies. When I got home I happened to be in my military collectible room where I have a World War II and Vietnam era collection of army uniforms and field gear. I happened to spy my Vietnam era army flak vest. It is a vest with lead inserts and leaded collar. It also has drawstrings on either side, as well as a front zipper.

I put it on and tightened the sides and zipped it up. At first it was very constricting but did an excellent job of mimicking an asthma attack. I would leave it on for ten minutes a day, getting used to the feeling and learning to control anxiety when I could not catch my breath. Amazingly, it did not take very long to feel relaxed in the vest. Besides calming my breathing fears, it also exercised my chest wall muscles to work harder, and thereby helped me to get stronger.

I began to look forward to my nightly self-help therapy. I increased the times from ten minutes to a couple of hours. My husband would remark that I had completed my therapy and it was OK to remove the vest. I balked at the idea of taking it off. What I did not realize at the time was that I had stumbled onto an excellent calming strategy for the autistic anxieties I experience. The deep pressure I

426877

AEP Connections
www.aepconnections.com
920-224-4794

DATE						

NAME

ADDRESS · ORDER NO.

CITY, STATE, ZIP

SOLD BY	CASH	C.O.D.	CHARGE	ON ACCT.	MDSE. RETD.	PAID OUT
	✗					

QUAN.		DESCRIPTION	PRICE	AMOUNT
1				
2				
3				
4				
5				
6				
7				
8				
9				
10				
11				
12				
13				
14				
RECEIVED BY			TAX	
			TOTAL	13.50

adams 24705

felt was comforting, relaxing, and instinctually craved. I now use it as a primary coping strategy when I get anxious or nervous.

Kids have a way of stumbling onto similar ideas when they carry heavy books in their book bag, even if they are not going to use the books in class that day. The weight of the backpack seems comforting and blends in well among peers. Some children find comfort wrapping themselves up tightly in a sleeping bag. Some like tight-fitting clothing but others do not. Weighted vests and blankets also produce a sense of calm for many, but not all, autistic individuals. It is important for calming strategies to be individually designed because of the diversity within the autistic community.

CALM

What first responders should *not* do

✘ Do not try to "reason" with an autistic individual in the midst of a catastrophic reaction.

✘ Do not tell individuals that they need to calm down. They know that and will as soon as they can.

✘ Do not ask a lot of questions.

✘ Do not have multiple responders making comments or asking questions.

✘ Do not ask what to do.

✘ Do not attempt to deceive the individual.

✘ Do not assume an aggressive posture.

✘ Do not use threats.

✘ Do not assume that a calming strategy that works with one autistic individual would work for another.

What first responders *should* do

✔ Remain calm. Just because the autistic individual has temporarily lost control of his/her behavior is no reason for you to do so.

✔ Identify one individual to interact with the individual who is temporarily distressed.

✔ Use simple declarative statements that affirm that you are there to assist the individual in regaining his/her composure.

✔ Ask for clarification. Ask the individual to repeat in his/her own words what he or she understands.

✔ Maintain a calm social presence until the crisis is over. The reaction is time-limited and it is counterproductive to try to rush recovery.

✔ Mirror the behavior of the individual in a way that shows compassion. If the individual is sitting on the ground rocking, it is more helpful to sit next to, rather than hover over, him or her.

✔ Determine if the individual has identification and an intervention plan.

Strategies autistic individuals can employ to remain calm

1. Include your calming strategies in your personalized intervention plan.

2. Assert your right to maintain your calming strategies when others insist that you drop them because they do not coincide with NT strategies. Sometimes you can modify them so that they do not stand out.

3. Develop new calming strategies. Often this will involve visual imagery. Sometimes it involves sensory focus.

4. Sometimes exercise can be helpful in developing body awareness so that strategies can be employed in a more timely fashion. Some individuals use a schedule to monitor their bodily state and adjust accordingly.

5. Music often can exert a calming influence. It can be helpful to use a walkman or MP3 player with calming music to assist in maintaining or restoring a calm mood.

Affirmation

Adult autistic individuals in our society have frequently been labeled as dysfunctional or broken. High-functioning autistic individuals have been out of sync with the rest of the population throughout their development. As a result they have not had positive affirmation from their peers. More often they have been the targets of abuse and exploitation. They are told that they need to be more like their peers, although their peers have been the source of much of their anguish. They are asked to deny their core being and conform to norms that they find unnatural at best and repugnant at worst.

"Friendly advice" is often not friendly and definitely not affirming. Most autistic individuals are trying very hard to be socially appropriate. It is a constant struggle due to the subtlety, hidden agendas, duplicity, and outright deceit that is common in everyday social interactions. They need feedback but sometimes it comes as a constant barrage, which only serves to diminish them as human beings.

Many autistic individuals have been misdiagnosed. This is especially true of adults. This is understandable because the diagnosis has not been available until recently. Many have been misplaced in mental hospitals or facilities for the retarded. Many more have not had the opportunity to fully make use of their talents.

Individuals who have not received positive affirmation of who they are, and who are constantly being told that they are defective, understandably have problems with low self-esteem.

Those individuals who have received positive affirmation from their family or a teacher or a friend have often made the most significant contributions in science and the arts.

Autistic individuals do not require the support of large numbers of people, but the support and trust of at least one individual can make a significant difference. A few individuals who provide unconditional acceptance, clear feedback, and support are invaluable. Often these individuals are not classmates but someone much older or younger who shares an interest.

Sometimes the only positive affirmation received is from a different species. Autistic individuals frequently develop close relationships with animals. Such a relationship can be extremely important in overcoming the effect of trauma.

As an adult, it is useful to have another adult who serves as a mentor. This can be in a chosen profession or line of work. It can also be someone who assists in understanding the unwritten rules of social engagement that autistic individuals find bewildering.

Lack of a positively affirming resource often leads to bad choices. False affirmation often comes disguised as benevolence. Autistic individuals can willingly accept the allure and promise of cults, drug traffickers, and radical groups.

The following is an example of the power of affirmation from when I was experiencing a meltdown. I write a column for the Autism Society of Maine newsletter and this account was initially printed there (March 2006) with a more humorous slant.

I frequently experience situations which, at the time, are frightening and lead to meltdowns. When I recover from the meltdown I feel a strong sense of humiliation and remorse. Some time later I am able to process what happened and try to view it in a humorous light. At the time it happens I am devastated.

Life is full of surprises, and surprises are not well received by many autistic individuals like me. As many of you know, I travel to various states doing an eight-hour seminar on autism and intervention strategies.

After a successful morning of presenting in Richmond, Virginia, I decided to end the morning session with the subject of unpredictability and novel situations that cause havoc to an autistic individual. I would pick up with the topic of meltdowns after lunch. I was feeling like a professional. People were impressed with my presenting style. I had the honor of having lunch with some of them in the hotel restaurant. There was a lot of noise all around that sounded to me like a swarming beehive. Still I decided to keep my composure and show my guests that I am an autistic who can function in such an environment. It was hard to focus on any one conversation. I had learned to pretend to pay attention when the noises became a sensory issue by every now and then interjecting "uh-huh" or a phrase like "that's interesting". I really was feeling in control, thinking, "What possibly could go wrong?" Then it happened...the unpredictable.

Halfway through our meal the hotel fire alarm went off. Blinding strobe lights and deafening sirens were all around me. Nobody moved. My traveling companion and I were the only ones to leave, which is what I was taught to do when a fire alarm goes off. No matter which way we went, the strobe lights and blaring horns were everywhere. I began to escalate and walk in tight circles. My companion implemented my intervention strategies, but there was no relief from the lights and sounds. As we went outside we were confronted with more flashing lights and sirens and the fire trucks arrived.

The alarms kept sounding for twenty minutes and we were told it was over. Just as we re-entered, the alarm system was reactivated and continued for another forty-five minutes. I was in complete meltdown and worried about my reputation. I thought my budding career on the lecture circuit had come to an end. Luckily the attendees had had a chance to get to know me as a person during the morning. Following the alarm a few came up and were very supportive. They had learned in the morning that I found my stuffed raccoon and the smell of leather calming. One attendee brought me my raccoon and another put her leather coat around me. That affirmation made all the difference in the world. Then, re-entering the room, still feeling ashamed and embarrassed, I received overwhelming applause by everyone in the room. It was an unintended but powerful teaching moment. Their affirmation gave me the strength I needed to regroup and deliver a powerful message on dealing with meltdowns.

Not only was this affirmation important to me, but I received feedback from several workshop participants that as a result of this experience they would be more comfortable if they were to encounter someone else experiencing a meltdown. The workshop ended with mutual affirmation.

I felt affirmation in that they accepted my meltdown as part of who I am. There were no negative or chiding remarks. The presentation of the stuffed raccoon and the leather coat was an acknowledgement of understanding my uniqueness in dealing with a terrible situation. My welcome back with applause meant the world to me. My distress was not minimized. In turn they received affirmation from me. Their empathy was acknowledged and they were affirmed for their support.

AFFIRMATION
What first responders should *not* do

✘ Do not assume that family members, acquaintances, caseworkers, or service providers are
   positive affirming resources.

✘ Do not assume, if an individual is not speaking,
   that he/she does not understand that he/she is
   being talked about.

✘ Do not talk about autistic individuals as if they
   are invisible.

✘ Do not overwhelm with many questions.

✘ Do not draw attention to perceived "bad behavior" such as swearing or threatening.

✘ Do not try to confront individuals and challenge the feelings of individuals in meltdown.
   They are not able to interpret or put their feelings in perspective but will more likely respond
   with "fear, freeze, or flee".

What first responders *should* do

✔ Refer to the autistic individual by name.

✔ Attempt to contact an individual that the autistic individual has identified as a trusted ally.

✔ Use acquaintances as translators to keep the autistic individual in control of the information.

✔ Make supportive statements indicating that you understand that the individual is stressed and state that your role is to stay with him/her until he/she gains composure, no matter how long it takes.

✔ Ask if the individual has an intervention plan. It should contain important biographical data defining who the individual is. Using that information, slowly interject descriptive comments such as "I see, your name is...", "You live at...", "Your best friend is your cat."

✔ Actively listen. Distressing feelings that are expressed, acknowledged, and validated by a trusted ally will diminish in intensity. Distressing feelings that are ignored will gain strength.

Strategies autistic individuals can employ to be seen as fellow human beings

1. Create and carry an identification card that includes your talents as well as your limitations.

2. Get to know first responders in your community so that they learn your gifts as well as your limitations.

3. Practice showing first responders your identification and intervention strategies.

4. Make sure your contact list contains the name of a trusted ally. Practice positive statements affirming who you are (and are not).

Routine

Everybody needs routine and predictability in order to function. For neurotypicals (NTs) routine is often primarily social, whether at work or play or within the family. NTs ritualistically involve cohorts in coffee/smoke breaks, travel arrangements, work projects, leisure activities, and all sorts of endeavors. The social network provides structure and safety for daily living. A disturbance in an individual routine may prove unsettling for a time but the multiplicity of the social network serves as a buffer against severe distress. Major social upheaval—for example, caused by a natural disaster or civil disturbance—may disrupt the whole social network and create extreme distress.

Routine for an autistic individual serves a similar function but is not socially based. Autistic routines tend to be narrow and focused. They are individualized and not generally shared by a community. They are often seen by NTs as dysfunctional patterns of behavior that need to be eliminated. Because the world is viewed as generally chaotic and unpredictable, routines play a major role in establishing a sense of control. Routines are commonly used as ways of entering or exiting social situations. During times of stress they are even more important and provide a main avenue of stress reduction. Routines reduce uncertainty. Ensuring consistency reduces anxiety. In adults the establishment of a schedule of everyday events can be helpful in avoiding being overwhelmed. Major tasks can sometimes be broken down into small doable activities that are scheduled throughout the day. Social events that are predictable, such as church services, are much more tolerable than more fluid events, such as parties.

Autistic individuals in supported living frequently have difficulty with changes from routine due to staff turnover. For autistic individuals, variety is not the spice of life. Sometimes staff feel that they are providing positive experiences by altering routine. A change in the breakfast menu, a new route to a day program, taking turns in choice of TV programming, all can increase stress and lead to unwanted results. Failure to consistently follow intervention strategies creates havoc.

Often autistic individuals have developed scripts that are potentially disastrous if followed. Scripts are fantasized routines that may be over-rehearsed if an individual has been restrained or had other negative experiences with first responders. Sometimes these scripts come from television and include flight or fight responses. It is common for individual scripts to involve fleeing to escape, or fighting. Possible scripts could include attempting to get a police officer's firearm. Sometimes these scripts are very public, in that the individual repeatedly makes statements about what he or she would do.

Routines or rituals are monotropic responses. While engaging in routines the individual is less likely to be able to incorporate new information. He or she may be receiving information from only one sensory modality.

The 3 R's—routine, ritual, and repetition—are very important to me and to other autistic individuals when we feel anxious, upset, or otherwise distressed. Unpredictability creates an undue amount of stress because we have a need to script every moment so that we feel in control, even if we are not. Routines are something we create that are very predictable and give us a sense of control. When stressed we resort to activities that are familiar and constant. In my case, I recently dealt with a great deal of stress working as a kayak guide. I would go to work expecting a tour and get there, only to find that my tour had no people, so I had no work. I had other tours in the afternoon, so I could not go home, and I was unprepared for the unscripted hours from morning till afternoon.

I needed to de-stress and I enjoy walking as a means to get calm. I would walk or pace back and forth along the beach for hours on end, frequently broadcasting my thoughts. This could lead others to think I was mentally deranged and in need of protective custody.

Inadvertently I began looking down and picking up interesting shiny objects. Very soon it became a ritual to search for sea glass while walking the beach. I would comb the stretch of beach again and again, as I always found something I missed the first few times around. It became very repetitive and as a result provided a sense of calming and a feeling that I had gained control over the unpredictable by doing something that was familiar. It was something that kept me focused (looking for sea glass), and was something predictable and constant and not subject to the change which is all around us. The stretch of beach was short, maybe fifty feet or so, but the walking back and forth looking for "treasure" was all that mattered. I would set goals for how many pieces I should find, and that, too, helped me to maintain the repetitiveness of walking such a short distance for hours on end.

This harmless routine marked by ritual and repetition staved off potential meltdowns for me. I looked like any other tourist searching for sea glass. When I am stressed and need to engage in such a routine, I want to be left alone. The distraction of someone talking or shadowing my every move only increases my anxiety level. At times like these, I need to be left alone. If not, it is perceived as an intrusion by an outsider. Autistic individuals are fearful that the routine or ritual that we have meticulously created will be messed up if someone attempts to intervene and we cannot predict his or her actions.

A slight deviation from routine, like walking a different path or going at a different pace, is enough to shatter our confidence in the effectiveness of a relied-on calming strategy. More harm is often done by someone just being "too close". The best intervention at times like these is to allow personal space.

If safety is an issue, use the least intrusive approach possible. Just remember that routine is the strategy that we employ frequently because it is the most effective tool that we have for reducing stress. Taking away that tool could easily precipitate greater risk. In this example, I was self-contained. There was little chance I would wander away from the beach and onto the street, because of my all-encompassing focus on finding sea glass. There was no sea glass to be found in the middle of a busy street.

Knowing when to intervene is frequently a difficult judgment call. It is important to use discretion and work with members of the autistic community in seeing routine as a source of strength in resolving chaotic situations.

ROUTINE

What first responders should *not* do

✗ Do not assume that a routine is an act of defiance.

✗ Do not interrupt a routine.

✗ Do not talk about the routine in a derogatory fashion.

✗ Do not try to talk an individual out of a routine.

What first responders *should* do

✔ If an individual is engaging in a routine he/she is already using a strategy to gain control over him- or herself. Reinforce the use of routine to gain calmness and control.

✔ Determine if the individual has an intervention plan that involves positive routines.

✔ One form of routine is the use of scripts to get through difficult situations. Find out if he/she has any such scripts.

✔ If an individual has positive scripts, gently try to incorporate them into the routine.

✔ Get to know individuals in the community and practice using positive scripts.

Strategies autistic individuals can employ to effectively use routine

1. Get to know first responders in your community and find out about routines that various first responders employ.

2. Develop scripts for different types of first responder interventions.

3. Practice routines with first responders and refer to your script.

4. Include a description of useful routines in your identification and intervention plan.

Empathy

It is often said and written that autistic individuals are deficient in the area of empathy. It is also claimed that they do not have a theory of mind (understanding what another person is thinking and feeling). Why is this? They are repeatedly told that they hurt others' feelings, thinking only about themselves, that they cannot see things from another's viewpoint. They are called self-absorbed, self-centered know-it-alls, who are incapable of having feelings.

Schools and churches are the main institutions designed to teach common values and social norms, where neurotypical (NT) individuals recognize the importance of a society based on conformity. Schools are one of the first places where socialization takes root, and the desire to "fit in" is prevalent with NT individuals. No one wants to be an outcast. Autistic individuals' social development is out of sync with the NTs'. They are not interested in being the same or accepted by others through conformity. The main motivation of NTs is to fit in and not be outcast. For autistics, not fitting in is not the problem. Bullying, teasing, and being abused in general are the problems. These are the unwritten consequences of not fitting in. After being continually subjected to such treatment, they sense that there is no point in even trying to fit in, and may isolate themselves even further from their age peers. This only causes more mistreatment and stigmatization as an outcast.

NTs enforce conformity in dress, thought, and action. They will shade the truth and be deceptive in order to fit in. Autistic individuals typically avoid their peer group. Because of their monotropic nature they do not integrate information from multiple sources. They tend to hear the words but miss the nonverbal cues.

In addition to that, they usually have a narrow definition of the words that they hear. They miss most of the communication that is not literal. They never develop the skills to recognize the subtle cues of social distress. For example, a person comes in not saying a word because they are depressed about something. There may be a "sad expression" on their face and an occasional sigh. If you ask them what is wrong they may say "nothing", but their nonverbal body language says otherwise. Autistic individuals may hear "nothing" and assume all is well because they are unable to pick up on the subtle body cues that say otherwise. They tend to favor honesty over political correctness. If being truthful and being polite are in conflict, they will generally opt for the truth. This leads to them making comments that are sometimes considered offensive. They are sometimes unaware of unwritten social conventions and codes of conduct because that is something picked up from peer integration and not from book learning.

Because of the stress placed on conformity, NT individuals are remarkably similar. Being able to know what someone else is thinking or feeling without him or her telling you is probably not a sixth sense, but rather it is only projection of one's thoughts and feelings onto another. Although this is stereotyping, it is a useful way of predicting the behavior of others. However, it is not useful in determining the thoughts and feelings of autistic individuals.

NTs frequently misinterpret an autistic person's action or reaction as a lack of caring what another person is feeling. The irony is that NT individuals who show no empathy towards autistic individuals judge autistic people as having no empathy. This is the real test of empathy: to understand the world of someone unlike you.

Autistic individuals are misjudged as having a lack of empathy. We appear to others as indifferent and even callous to another's unfortunate circumstance because we don't react in the way that non-autistic people do. Empathy manifests itself in many different ways.

For example, as a licensed wildlife rehabilitator I rehabbed my first bat this past winter. Initially I was creeped out by the thing due to years of watching Dracula movies, and I had a hard time because I had preconceived notions about bats being evil. As I told those around me that I was working with a bat they began to say horrible, untrue things about bats, believing that they had no useful purpose on earth. They were working on stereotypes and "old wives' tales". Once I realized that this poor bat was misjudged, not on its merits, but from folklore, I felt protective toward it and my fears vanished. I could identify (empathize) with what it feels like to be negatively stereotyped. This is often what happens to me when I tell a stranger I am autistic. I identified with the bat. To me that is true empathy, to understand another being from his or her perspective.

Empathy does not mean that we have to give an emotional response to show that we understand or even care. I was invited out to dinner with a friend and her autistic child. She decided on a fast-food joint because her young child liked the chicken nuggets at this place. It was lunchtime and I was apprehensive because of the sensory issues that occur when walking into a busy fast-food place. My friend assured me we would not have to wait long to get our lunch because they process orders very quickly. I had some concerns also for the young child, but then thought that my friend was more knowledgeable about her son and his sensory issues. I went along with the plan because I did not want to seem difficult or "picky" to my friend. As we stepped into the packed place, the buzzing noise of the people was extremely loud.

I had all I could do to try to contain myself with the noise, the lighting, and people crowding me from all sides. It was hard for my friend to understand why even five minutes is unbearable to autistic people who have sensory issues, because her sensory experience is entirely different. I turned to the young child and saw such an agonizing pitiful look. I understood what he was feeling because I was experiencing the same feelings. It seemed that we were the only two people there who were finding the experience torturous. The young child then covered his ears and began yelling loudly and then broke down crying. Within seconds it progressed to a full-blown catastrophic reaction. I was overcome with empathy because I could identify exactly with how this child was feeling. I was experiencing the same sensory overload and could easily respond in the same fashion. My friend froze because she did not know what had caused the reaction and she was embarrassed in front of the other patrons. I did not say a word or show any emotion, but I scooped that little child up in my arms and rushed outside of the building where we could both de-stress. My response was based on empathy. To the casual observers my actions could easily have been misinterpreted. They may have empathized with the mother and may have seen my actions as designed to relieve the mother's embarrassment.

Autistic individuals are under constant pressure to empathize with NTs. When we try it is usually misinterpreted. As a result we find it easier to empathize with the outcasts because we understand what that feels like. We find it easier to show empathy for animals and disenfranchised people. We may even empathize too much with some people. We are attracted to and empathize with other autistic individuals and with other humans who have faced rejection. We cry over abused animals and people with whom we can identify.

We do have emotions and feelings. They are just not expressed in the same way. We laugh, we cry, and we feel pain and sorrow just like everyone else. What we need is a little empathy from society to recognize that there is more than one way (the norm) to express compassion and feelings.

EMPATHY

What first responders should *not* do

✗ Do not assume that autistic individuals do not have powerful feelings.

✗ Do not lecture them about how their behavior scares others.

✗ Do not interpret presenting behaviors as an accurate reflection of their feelings.

✗ Do not take everything they say personally; it often is not about you.

✗ Do not ask them what they are feeling. For most autistic individuals it is very difficult to describe feelings. Pressuring them to do so will only increase their stress.

✗ Do not minimize what they are experiencing or belittle their behaviors.

✗ Do not demand eye contact.

What first responders *should* do

✔ Determine if the individual has an intervention plan that involves empathic interventions.

✔ Show empathy and compassion by reassuring individuals and letting them know that they are not alone. Acknowledge and validate their fear.

✔ Make statements that you personally know how it feels to be scared.

✔ Accept the individual non-judgmentally.

✔ Individuals trying to resolve their catastrophic reactions sometimes find comfort in hearing their own words reflected back to them.

✔ Use a clear, low voice.

✔ Mirror physical behavior. Observe and match the person's motions and emotions in a sensitive fashion. Done with empathy, mirroring can be effective in helping to create trust.

✔ Understand that the behavior has meaning and may be a sign of the need to express unmodulated emotion or regain emotional control.

✔ Touch should be offered but not forced.

Strategies autistic individuals can employ to encourage empathy

1. Get to know first responders in your community and find out about how they provide assistance to marginalized or helpless people.

2. Tell first responders that you have concern for the helpless and abused. Ask them how they intervene with such individuals. This will allow the autistic individual and first responders to positively engage, leading each to be seen by the other in a positive light.

3. Learn about the connection that your behaviors have to your emotions, and communicate that to others so that you will not be misunderstood.

4. Remind yourself constantly that first responders are there to help and not hurt you.

5. Identify contact people who have an empathic understanding of you and can communicate that to others.

Develop a Plan

Everyone who experiences catastrophic reactions needs to have a plan for handling them in ways that do not lead to further complications. Neurotypicals (NTs) typically have unwritten plans that include contacting friends and family members for support. Autistic individuals benefit from a written plan that is communicated to first responders, because their needs in times of crisis are different.

For some autistic individuals, catastrophic reactions are severely debilitating. They may occur many times a day, most days of their lives. The sensory and cognitive changes may mean that they are frequently at risk. If appropriate intervention is not available they may put others at risk as well.

For others the risk of harm to self or others is minimal. The overwhelming stimulation may lead to withdrawal to a safe place or position. They may stop talking or eating, or neglect hygiene, but are not a safety risk.

Catastrophic reactions are time-limited, but appropriate interventions can reduce the likelihood of turning a challenging situation into a tragic one.

Each plan will be unique and dependent on many factors.

Individuals differ in terms of how a meltdown is experienced and how that experience is displayed in overt behavior. Some individuals get stuck in a "freeze" mode and become immobilized. Sometimes this results in responding to any question by saying, "no" or "why?" Other individuals may flee to a safe place. Others again may show less obvious outward signs that they are experiencing a meltdown. A mathematics professor may become immobilized when confronted with departmental politics.

Individuals also differ in their support systems. Some live alone while others live in highly structured supportive environments. Some are well integrated into their community and are well acquainted with a variety of likely first responders. Some have had no contact or have had negative experiences with the police, fire department, or hospital emergency room personnel.

Plans may be very simple and straightforward or quite complex. An example of a simple plan might be to place a sign/placard in a autistic child's bedroom to alert first responders in case of an emergency. First responders in the community could be notified of the child's likely behavior in an emergency, i.e. hides under his bed, becomes mute, etc. For an adult with a history of trauma, there may be many subtle triggering stimuli requiring a more extensive knowledge of the individual. There are some situations that I know are likely to lead to meltdowns despite all my prevention strategies. For my own personal plan I wear around my neck a passport holder with a clear window. Through the window in large letters read "I HAVE AUTISM". In smaller letters are instructions to open and read in case of emergency. Contained inside is the name and telephone number of a contact person who knows my intervention strategies and can help clarify what needs to be done. Also contained is a one page crisis intervention plan.

In each case there are some factors common to each plan:

- *Identification.* It is important to identify the individual having a catastrophic reaction as autistic. It is strongly recommended that the individual carry an identification card. There are a number of identification cards available through different organizations. In the US most state associations provide safety aids including IDs. We recommend making your own custom ID (see www.selectautismmerchandise.com, www.okparentnetwork.org, www.autismsource.org and www.mypreciouskid.com). Most list essential contact information, as well as brief descriptions of stressors, meltdowns, and interventions. It is also important to identify the catastrophic reaction for what it is and not a psychotic break, a seizure, or a drug reaction.

- *Concrete.* The wording of the plan needs to be descriptive and not evaluative. By being precise, evaluative assumptions can be avoided and first responders will have the benefit of a clear and common language. Describe what the meltdown looks like, using simple terms. The first approximation of a plan should be very basic and accurate as it is easier to add details to the plan than change exisiting details.

- *Communication of plan.* Although first responders are likely to ask for identification, they are less likely to expect an intervention plan. Failure to communicate the existence of a plan means that first responders will use existing protocols. Sometimes it is possible to make first responders in the community aware of potential catastrophic reactions. Teachers, police, firefighters, physicians, crisis workers, case workers, and emergency room personnel are all possible first responders who can be made aware of a history of catastrophic reactions. If they have a written plan it leads to more appropriate interventions.

- *Rehearsal of interventions.* It usually is not sufficient to have a written plan. During crises, people, including first responders, revert to conventional responses. It helps to practice interventions preparatory to the need to implement them. It also helps for the autistic individual to have scripted and practiced responses which would assist first responders. This might include something as simple as presenting one's identification. This seems intuitive, but for many autistic individuals the first reaction is to freeze. If control is not regained it is likely followed by a flight or fight response.

- *Revising plans.* Revising a plan can be a difficult undertaking. Autistic individuals have difficulty with change. They often prefer a predictable event, though it may be counterproductive. It is best to start with simple, clear, effective, well-practiced strategies. That may initially consist of only displaying an identification card on request. It is necessary to revise plans when they do not work or are no longer sufficient. It is generally easier to add components to a plan, as opposed to removing them. Plans also evolve as individuals develop more effective coping strategies. It is important to reevaluate the plan frequently and modify existing strategies as conditions warrant.

DEBORAH LIPSKY'S PERSONAL INTERVENTION PLAN

I have had a series of terrible experiences with first responders. At times, the experiences led to catastrophic reactions. At other times, I was in the middle of a catastrophic reaction and those around me did not know how to react.

So, I developed a plan.

INTERVENTION STRATEGIES FOR DEB LIPSKY IN CASE OF MELTDOWN OR ESCALATION OF BEHAVIORS (ONCE STARTED I NEED YOUR INTERVENTION TO STOP)

1. Constantly use my name with a firm tone and redirect my attention by saying, "It's OK Deb." Don't stop until this is accomplished. (Like a phone ringing, it sometimes takes a few "rings" to pick up on my name being repeated.)

2. A firm grip on my shoulder while redirecting me is 99% effective. Think of it as waking me up out of a bad dream. Physical contact grounds me back to reality.

3. NEVER try to reason, give lengthy explanations, teach new coping skills, or ask me open-ended questions while I am in an agitated state.

NEVER LEAVE ME UNATTENDED UNTIL I HAVE CALMED DOWN.

WARNING SIGNS OF ESCALATION

1. repeating myself. Saying a word or phrase over and over is the start of an episode

2. trouble answering questions and/or stuttering, accompanied by a puzzled look

3. sharp reduction in eye contact or focusing ability

4. increase in intensity of rocking, hand/body movements

5. impulsively getting up and walking in tight circles

6. complete communication shutdown. Sudden stop in verbalization means conflict turned inward and escalation process still continuing (even though you do not see it).

Moderate/high anxiety state means a high risk of injury due to:

1. being unaware of surroundings—inability to spot dangers

2. physical fatigue from energy expended increasing motor clumsiness

3. high pain threshold—do not feel pain until it is really severe

4. tendency to wander or flee from situation.

KEEP IN MIND: I comprehend next to nothing of what is going on at the time. After I de-escalate, make sure that I am safe before allowing me to leave. Ask me questions to ensure my cognitive awareness is back. Write down any important instructions, tasks, or things for me to remember later on.

Moderate anxious states occur primarily due to:

1. not understanding reason for sudden change

2. not getting understandable answers to my questions

3. people in charge of my care not explaining the process

4. being taken by surprise—caught off guard.

PLEASE! NEVER LEAVE ME UNATTENDED UNTIL I HAVE CALMED DOWN!

Having spent time and effort developing this plan you might think things got easier for me. I routinely gave this plan to professional service providers, friends, and acquaintances. In spite of this, the plan was sometimes ignored. At other times implementation was inconsistent. It was all very frustrating. Crisis workers and ER personnel felt that they knew best. On one visit to the ER following an insect bite (I had an allergic reaction) I asked the nurse to contact a friend because under stress communication breaks down. My contacts are listed on my identification. She did, and that greatly facilitated the situation. When it was time to be seen by the doctor, he denied my request, stating that he knew how to handle the situation. Luckily I was accompanied, or the situation could have led to a full-scale catastrophic reaction.

It is essential that a first responder stay in my visual field during a meltdown. If not, he or she ceases to exist for me. This means being within four feet of me and to my side. I rely on peripheral vision, and when stressed do not see directly in front of me. I cannot make eye contact in most situations. Forced eye contact when stressed makes matters much worse.

Even for those who know me quite well, it is essential that we review and rehearse meltdown strategies. It helps to practice having someone firmly press on my shoulders. What is a firm touch for one person is a light touch for someone else. Practice makes both of us more comfortable with interventions.

We all change as we experience positive relationships and learn to trust. As others get to know and understand us, catastrophic reactions become less frequent. We learn to trust some people to be able to anticipate difficulties and to respond appropriately.

As those around us get to know about catastrophic reactions, they become more skillful and less apprehensive. When around some people with whom I am comfortable, meltdowns rarely occur. Even when they do occur due to some unforeseen event, I am comfortable that the situation would be resolved easily. When I am around other people, meltdowns occur very frequently. I try to prepare myself and develop avoidance or escape strategies.

Reviewing and modifying a plan can be extremely difficult. Some of us have difficulty with change and prefer a known approach that does not work to a changed approach that is more likely to be successful. It took me quite a while to revisit this plan, even though what would appear to be a minor modification was all that was needed.

DEVELOP A PLAN

What first responders should *not* do

✗ Do not ignore my identification card.

✗ Do not ignore my request to contact a trusted individual.

✗ Do not assume, because you have received crisis intervention training, that you understand my needs during a catastrophic reaction.

What first responders *should* do

✔ Ask for identification. Do so in a straightforward manner. When asked "Do you have indentification?" an autistic individual may respond "Yes" without handing it over and return to self-stimming behavior. A more direct request would be "Show me your identification so I can help you."

✔ Affirm the individual by responding to requests consistent with the plan. Validate the individual by acknowledging the plan and adhering to its specifics.

✔ If the individual has no plan, once the crisis is over assist the individual in developing a plan.

✔ If the plan is used successfully, affirm the helpfulness of the plan.

✔ If there were difficulties implementing the plan, follow up with the individual to assist in revising the plan.

Strategies autistic individuals can employ in developing a plan

1. Take charge in implementing, monitoring, and revising a plan.

2. Make your plan available to anyone who might need to know. This might include new friends, supervisors, clergy, as well as the usual first responders.

3. Rehearse your plan with others when at all possible. This provides needed clarification.

4. Revise and modify your plan as needed.